Selecting

A Nursing Home

Helping You Make The Right Decision

Selecting

A Nursing Home

Helping You Make The Right Decision

By

Kathleen M. O'Toole, RN, BSN

ISBN: 1-58820-210-0

This guide is dedicated to senior adults and their families who have reached a particular crossroad in life. It is not a substitute for qualified, professional assistance but it may serve as a useful guide in helping to make one of life's more difficult decisions.

Special thanks goes to those who contributed to the writing, editing and production of this guide, especially my wonderful husband. Your input and support were greatly appreciated.

Table of Contents

Commonly Asked Questions 73

This section will help you by providing the answers to commonly asked questions. In addition, we provide some of the questions that you can expect to be asked by the nursing home you have selected

Terminology Made Easy 89

During this time you will come across many new terms that you may not be familiar with. This glossary will provide helpful definitions to increase your understanding.

Places To Turn For Additional Help 93

Suggestions are provided for identifying additional resources that you can contact on a national, state or local level for assistance and information.

Recommended Reading 95

Additional reading is suggested that can help you through this time.

From The Author...

Dear Reader,

Thank you for selecting this guide. I realize that you now face the difficulties associated with making one of life's more important decisions. Whether time is on your side or not, you want to spend your time effectively making an informed and confident decision. The intent of this guidebook is to help you do just that.

The reality is that the luxury of time in making the decision is most likely not on your side. This guidebook is made accessible because many books cover this topic from a theoretical standpoint rather than a practical one. What you need to know is how to begin, what the major steps are along the way and finally, how to make the best decision that supports a quality and dignity of life for a loved one.

Selecting A Nursing Home is not meant to take a very important decision in life and make it seem simple. It is, however, designed to help you through the entire process by organizing thoughts, information and time for you and your loved one. This is not an easy time in anyone's life. It can be filled with emotional stress, uncertainty and frustration. This guide is ready to go to work for you. My ultimate goal is to help you make an informed decision ... a decision that you and your loved one can live with.

Sincerely,

Kathleen M. O'Toole, RN, BSN

How To Use This Guide

Selecting A Nursing Home is a tool that will guide and counsel you, help you think through important issues and answer questions. The information provided is designed to help individuals looking for a nursing home for themselves, a loved one or a friend. However, to maintain consistency throughout, the wording is from the perspective of the family members who are helping their loved one.

It is important to keep in mind that there is no set amount of time that it will take you to select the right nursing home. This guide will help you keep organized and, ultimately, help you through the process effectively. How long it will take depends on many factors. Time may be working against you. Because of the importance of the decision, you will want to designate appropriate time that may range from just a few days to several weeks. The sooner you begin and the more organized and prepared you are, the sooner an informed decision can be made.

We suggest, as a beginning, to identify other family members who should be part of the decision making process. This is not a time to act alone. You will want to include your loved one, whom the decision will most affect, as well as other family members. It may be more difficult to get agreement from others in the family as you address each question or issue, but ultimately the input and open dialogue will be healthy. Even if key family members seem impartial or if there are distance constraints, work hard at soliciting their input.

As you use this guide, you will see practical worksheets and forms designed to generate and capture your thoughts and plans. You may want to write your personal notes and comments on the pages. Feel free to use this guide as your journal.

To get the most out of this guide, scan through it in its entirety before completing any of the worksheets. You will get a general overview of the types of worksheets, forms and information that are provided and a feel for the entire process you will be going through.

You are ready to proceed!

Are There Alternatives?

Before you begin your nursing home search, it is best to have an overview of adult care alternatives. Many people head down the nursing home path without realizing the many alternatives that exist. If you are confident that a nursing home is the best alternative, then proceed to page 17, "Identifying Needs and Desires". However, if you are not sure or if the primary care physician has not already ordered a service for your loved one, it is wise to determine what needs require outside-of-the-family assistance. Use this section to guide you in determining your loved one's level of assistance so that an appropriate adult care service can be selected.

Deciding on the appropriate adult care service for your loved one begins by determining the level of assistance required. Assistance is defined for our purposes as help given to an individual by an able person to perform and complete tasks that can not be completed independently. The eleven (11) areas of assistance, as accepted by the medical community, are activities of daily living:

Dressing	**Bathing**
Toileting	**Eating**
Preparing a meal	**Driving**
Handling finances	**Shopping**
Using a telephone	**Housekeeping**
Taking medication	

The following worksheets on pages 3 and 4 are provided to help you understand and decide what alternatives may be able to assist your loved one to complete these activities of daily living.

Begin with Worksheet A on page 3 to help you determine the level of required assistance. To use Worksheet

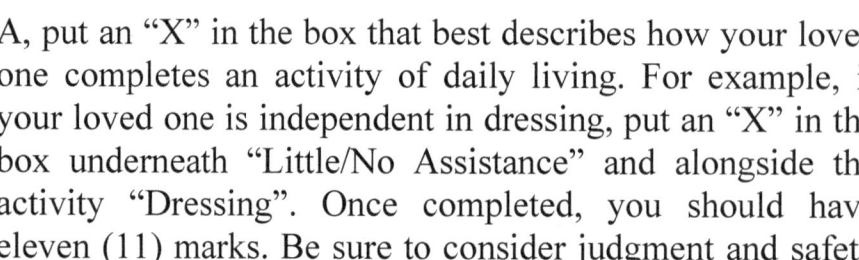

A, put an "X" in the box that best describes how your loved one completes an activity of daily living. For example, if your loved one is independent in dressing, put an "X" in the box underneath "Little/No Assistance" and alongside the activity "Dressing". Once completed, you should have eleven (11) marks. Be sure to consider judgment and safety of performing each task before deciding on the level of assistance. For example, a person may be physically capable of driving a car, yet safety is compromised because his judgment is impaired. Once you have completed worksheet A, examine what you see to determine what activities require the most assistance.

Worksheet A

Determining Level of Required Assistance

Selecting the appropriate adult care service begins with recognizing one's level of assistance required to accomplish activities of daily living. Place an "X" in the box that corresponds with your loved one's level of required assistance in performing each of these activities. Once the level of assistance is determined, compare it to the Adult Care Services Matrix on page 4.

Activities of daily living:	Levels of Required Assistance:		
	Little/No Assistance	Moderate Assistance	Complete Assistance
Dressing			
Bathing			
Toileting			
Preparing a meal			
Eating			
Handling finances			
Driving			
Using a telephone			
Shopping			
Taking Medication			
Housekeeping			

Once you have completed this worksheet, proceed to the next page, the Adult Care Services matrix. This will help you match the assistance level that you identified here for your loved one with those of the fifteen (15) adult care services available in most communities.

Adult Care Services Matrix

This matrix illustrates the 15 types of adult care services available in most communities. Associated with each is the level of "Assistance" that is appropriate for that service. Match the level of assistance that you identified for your loved one on Worksheet A with those recommended here to determine the appropriate adult care service alternative.

Adult Care Service Alternatives:	Levels of Required Assistance:		
	Little/No Assistance	Moderate Assistance	Complete Assistance
Independent living at home	X		
Home with telephone service	X		
Home with part-time companion	X		
Home with Homemaker	X		
Home with delivered meals	X		
Senior Center	X		
Foster Care	X		
Congregate housing	X		
Live-in companion	X	X	
Assisted Living	X	X	
Adult day care	X	X	X
Home care Nurse/Aide		X	X
Nursing Home		X	X
Respite care		X	X
Hospice care		X	X

Review pages 5-9 for an explanation of each of these adult care service alternatives.

Once you have completed Worksheet A, examine what you see to determine what activities require the most assistance.

Defining Available Services

Let us define each of the adult care service alternatives listed on page 4, the "Adult Care Services Matrix", to give you an understanding of each.

Independent Living At Home - Persons in this category are able to care for themselves and do not necessarily require assistance to complete their activities of daily living.

Telephone Service (living at home) - In some areas, organizations exist which will place prearranged telephone calls to remind persons to take medication, to determine if they have safely transferred out of bed for the day or that they have safely prepared themselves for bed. In some cases, family members can provide this function. Another telephone service is a Life-Call or Emergency Response system in which a person wears a necklace or wrist ornament that has a button to press if the person is in need of immediate emergency attention.

Home With Part-Time Companion - A service that offers a qualified person who may be authorized to perform a variety of tasks or only a few tasks. These tasks may consist of any or all of the following:

Visiting with your loved one
Taking her/him for walks
Providing transportation for errands or appointments
Providing housekeeping or meal preparation assistance.

The service often depends on two factors - the client's needs and the agency's description of "companion service".

Home With Homemaker - An individual who comes in to your home who is capable of performing housekeeping duties as decided by the client and the policies of the servicing agency.

Home With Delivered Meals - A service offered by local organizations such as Visiting Nurse Agencies or local church groups. The meals are usually offered for a minimal daily charge and are delivered to the client's home. Diet restrictions are respected.

Senior Center - Most communities have a senior center which ***is*** often associated with the town's community center. A senior center offers a variety of recreational and educational programs designed to meet the social needs of senior community members. Programs vary from community to community and are based on the economic situation of each center. Transportation to and from the center varies and may or may not be offered by the center. Membership requirements differ for each center. Call the Town (City) Clerk's office for details concerning a senior center in your community.

Foster Care - An organization that matches needs and desires of an individual with a family who meets qualification criteria in caring for that person in their home. Once a match is found, the individual requiring the care moves in and becomes a part of that family.

Congregate Housing - An apartment or condominium-like facility offering a living environment for the adult population. Many offer recreational activities, laundry facilities, and one meal a day in a dining room. Health care services vary among facilities. Some offer nursing services on a daily basis but not on a twenty-four (24) hour basis. Transportation services are usually offered by each facility. The specifics regarding the usage of the transportation service vary. Fees for residing in a congregate housing unit differ for each provider and are based on the number and types of services offered to the residents.

Live-in Companion - Anyone who requires little to moderate assistance and wishes to live at home and has the finances to afford a live-in companion, may want to contact a local agency that offers this service. A live-in companion can be a housekeeper who prepares meals, cleans the home, launders the clothes and linens while providing companionship. This person, if needed, can be a certified nurses aide able to provide personal care to satisfy activities of daily living needs and to perform the duties that the housekeeping companion performs.

Assisted living - An apartment-like setting in which the individual requires little to moderate assistance with the activities of daily living by a home health aide or nurses aide. Nursing staff is available twenty-four (24) hours a day. The facility commonly offers more than one meal a day, usually lunch and dinner in a communal dining area.

Adult Day Care - A service that benefits those families who are capable and willing to care for their loved one at home in the evenings and on weekends but are unable to care for them during the work day. The Adult Day Care provides care and activities through the day. Activities vary from center to center. The staff usually consists of a nurse, social service workers and recreational technicians who provide the activities. Transportation to and from the day care is generally provided by the center. Breakfast and lunch are usually served. Each center has a maximum number of people that it can accommodate. Some serve a group as small as ten or twenty while larger centers can serve up to eighty people. It is important to know if your loved one likes small or large groups and if your loved one likes to interact in a group or likes to be with one person. This knowledge can help you make the right fit between the center and your loved one.

Home Care - Provided by a community or town based visiting nurse association or a home health care agency. Each of these organizations offers nursing and home health aide services. The agencies have state and federal guidelines that mandate the type of care they provide. The quality of the care is determined by the satisfaction of the client and by the internal quality assurance program of each agency. Some agencies offer other medical services such as physical therapy, occupational therapy, speech therapy, social service assistance, specialty nursing services such as maternal-child, psychiatric, cardiac, diabetes and pediatrics. Housekeeping and companion services may also be offered.

Nursing Home - These services can be found under several titles such as: Health Care Center, Rehabilitation Center, Long-term Care Facility (LCF), or Short-term Care Facility (SCF). Some facilities stay with the original namesakes of Nursing Home or Convalescent Home. Whatever title is used for a facility of your choice, the basic services are the same. These facilities provide around-the-clock skilled nursing care for their residents. Care is classified as short- or long-term care. Short-term care is usually for those requiring rehabilitation of some kind and who will be able to advance to other living arrangements. Long-term care is provided to those who will require ongoing skilled care and living assistance. Some facilities have a specialty such as pulmonary rehabilitation. Identify the specialty of the nursing home of choice and determine if the care given under that specialty is appropriate in relation to meeting your loved one's needs.

Respite Care - This service can come in many forms: a nurse, a home health aide, or a part-time or live-in companion. Respite care can even be in the form of a short-term stay in a nursing home. If you have a loved one who lives with you and cannot be left alone while you go on vacation, respite care can be offered by a nursing home, a home care agency or any agency that offers companion services. It is best to discuss this with your physician especially if your loved one requires skilled medical attention. A nurse or certified nurses aide may be required as opposed to a companion who is an unlicensed person.

Hospice Care - This care is offered to any individual regardless of age who requires skilled nursing care and has an illness that the physician has documented to be terminal with six (6) months or less to live. This service can be provided by an independent hospice organization, a visiting nurse or home health care agency, or a hospital based program.

These are the most commonly utilized services that are available in most communities to support the growing needs of the adult population. To get additional information about these and other services that may become available in your community, contact your local social worker or one of the organizations identified on page 93 of this guidebook.

Understanding Payer Sources

One of the main concerns of nursing home care is paying the fees. At this early point in your nursing home search, it is important to understand how you or your loved one will pay the cost of care. The ideal situation is to plan ahead. If your loved one's physical condition is making independent living more of a challenge and you are considering what kind of care will be needed in the future, then you may want to plan ahead to cover the cost of care.

The first place to start is to figure out your loved one's assets. Investment plans or portfolios, insurance policies, a home and a car are a few samples of assets. They can be used towards the payment of nursing home care. This is the time to consult with an estate planner or elder law attorney. These experts can give you financial advice in regards to preparing for future health care costs. Plan a meeting with an expert and include your   loved one and all key-decision-making family members.

For some people, discussing finances can be a very sensitive issue. It is important that your loved one know in advance that full disclosure of the financial situation to the expert is necessary. Be sure that all involved, especially your loved one, are comfortable with the expert chosen.

The process may take months to complete depending on the financial status of your loved one. Often times, it is necessary to obtain past bank statements or past statements from other asset sources. These requests may take weeks to obtain and may require a fee. Write down each contact you make with an asset source and the results of your discussion. This process will help you keep track of which organization is sending what document and when.

Planning ahead helps to eliminate the stress and worry of paying for the future care of your loved one. Though this process can be a sensitive and emotional topic for many individuals and families, it is an important step in life to provide for a secure future.

If time is not on your side and nursing home placement is necessary immediately, then financial consultation can be arranged once your loved one is securely placed in a nursing home. Some financial guidance can be obtained from hospital social workers or discharge personnel. The staff of the financial department in a nursing home can give you guidance as well, but it may be limited to your present situation. For future planning for the cost of care, consult with an estate planner or elder law attorney.

It is common knowledge that the average nursing home will cost between $4,500 to $6,000 a month for a semi-private two person room. Additional costs may exist in the form of physician visits, therapist visits and, possibly, medications. With these additions, the cost of care rises.

A payer source is an accessible fund to use towards the cost of health care. Payer sources for health care can consist of:

- Medicare (Title 18)
- Medicaid or state welfare health plan
- private insurance/long-term care insurance plans
- cash or out-of-pocket funds

Each source has specific rules, regulations, requirements and restrictions which determine eligibility and reimbursement. Your loved one's age, physical, and financial situation will determine which payor source is appropriate.

Medicare

Consider medicare as a payer source. Medicare offers health insurance coverage for citizens over the age of 65. Part A Medicare pays for hospitalization costs and certain tests and procedures. Part B Medicare, which is a supplement paid for by the beneficiary, covers home care costs and physician bills. Medications are not presently covered under medicare. Medicare disability is a similar package which covers disabled persons under the age of 65. A physician determines disability and files the necessary paperwork.

At present, medicare covers skilled care in a nursing facility for a variety of illnesses and diseases, primarily rehabilitation, for a limited number of days. Admission into the nursing home must occur within 30 days of a hospitalization otherwise medicare will not consider paying for the charges. Occasionally a co-payment is incurred depending on the nature of the admission and medicare's regulations. The facility's billing department will be able to answer any questions you have concerning medicare regulations

Keep in mind that medicare is in a state of flux. This means that the rules, regulations and requirements may change or may have already changed. For the most current information regarding medicare reimbursements, it is best to contact your nearest medicare office.

Medicaid or state welfare health plan

Another payer source, is Medicaid or a state's welfare health plan. Many states recognize this plan as medicaid while others, such as the state of California, recognize this plan under another name. The name for this type of insurance may differ between states as well as the qualifications. In general, requirements are that an individual must have a maximum allowed monthly income which is established by the state (an amount normally below the poverty level) and may not have assets, such as a house, a car, even stocks or a life insurance policy. Note that some states allow an individual to maintain assets but liens are placed against them. States also have different requirements depending on whether an individual or couple is involved. Earnings made from the sale of the home or car or insurance policy would be used towards the cost of nursing home care before application for medicaid is possible. Once on medicaid, an individual will be able to receive care in a nursing home that accepts medicaid reimbursement. A good medicaid resource person would be an estate planner or an elder law attorney. Discussion of your situation with one of these specialists will give you an idea if your loved one qualifies for state welfare health insurance.

Private insurance/Long-term care insurance plans

A third payer source is an active insurance plan that contains benefits for long-term care. Review your loved one's insurance policy or policies for any such benefit. Since the increase of nursing home admissions, insurance companies now offer policies specifically for covering nursing home care. Be sure to review any plan thoroughly to understand all requirements and regulations before purchasing a plan. If you are unsure of a plan, consult with an estate planner for help.

Cash or out-of-pocket funds

The last payer source is cash or out-of-pocket funds. These are monies your loved one may have in the form of assets. If you are in a situation in which your loved one must pay for nursing home care without the assistance of any other payer source, be sure to consult with an estate planner or an elder law attorney. These specialists will be able to help you determine what assets are available, any associated tax implications and how to plan for paying nursing home costs.

Be sure to have a clear understanding of your loved one's financial situation. Once you fully understand what finances are available then you can determine which payer source is best for you. Consulting with the hospital and nursing home social workers, if your loved one is presently hospitalized, is a good place to start. If you can arrange a meeting with an estate planner or elder law attorney you will be able to understand the financial laws that apply in your state. Planning ahead for nursing home care or other health care your loved one may need is the best insurance anyone can have.

Identifying Needs and Desires

Selecting the right nursing home begins here. Before spending valuable time visiting several different facilities, take time to identify the needs and desires of your loved one. In other words, what you are looking for in a nursing home. Identifying what you and your loved one desires from a nursing home will guide you in the questions to ask each facility that you visit.

Too often, individuals and their families select a nursing home only to later identify issues they wish they had known of or should have looked for, such as:

How desirable is the location of the nursing home?

What specific skilled care is provided?

Is being on a bus route important for family members to visit the nursing home?

Do the activities or hobbies provided meet your loved one's desires and expectations?

These are just some issues you will want to identify before you start looking at nursing homes. Remember, it is important to identify what the specific needs and desires of your loved one are in order to find the nursing home that can satisfy those   needs and desires. Identifying what you are looking for before you start your search will help ensure that your loved one's new home is the right home.

On the following pages are worksheet #1 (pages 19-25) and worksheet #2 (pages 26-32) called "Identifying Needs and Desires". Complete worksheet #1 and have your loved one complete worksheet #2. It is important to include your loved one, as well as other key family members. These decisions affect the whole family; include them in the decision making process. This will help everyone through the transition.

Once you have completed the "Identifying Needs and Desires" worksheets, compare and discuss your answers. Once you understand and agree with each other, you will be better able to work together in searching for the right nursing home.

Worksheet #3 is the copy for you to collect the agreed upon choices from worksheets #1 and #2. Keep the section titled "Nursing Home Comparisons" blank for now as it will be used once you begin visiting several different nursing homes. These pages will ultimately show the needs and desires that each nursing home can satisfy.

Once you have completed worksheet #3, proceed to page 41, the "Nursing Home Learning Tool".

Identifying Needs and Desires
Worksheet #1

Your Name: _____

Date Completed: _____

This worksheet should be completed by the responsible family member(s) participating in the selection process of the nursing home. Another copy of the survey is on pages 26-32 and should be completed by the loved one requiring the assistance of the nursing home.

Each worksheet contains headings, an incomplete sentence, and a group of needs and desires. Review each section. Place an "I", an "S" or an "N" on each space in the boxes provided as the statement pertains to your needs and desires.

Use a letter **I** for important
Use a letter **S** for somewhat important
Use a letter **N** for not important

I. Facility Location
(This group of statements pertains to the
location of a desirable health care facility)

	It is **I**mportant, **S**omewhat important, or **N**ot important for the nursing home location to be...
	near family/friends
	near primary physician for easy access to appointments
	near hospital of your choice
	near preferred house of worship

Additional Comments:

I. Facility Location - Continued

It is **I**mportant, **S**omewhat important, or **N**ot important for the nursing home location to be...	
	near shopping center
	access to public transportation
	suburban (rural) location
	on busy street

Additional Comments:

II. Resident Room
(This group of statements pertains to the
desirable personal room environment)

It is Important, Somewhat important, or Not important to have...	
	a private room (single occupancy)
	a semi-private room (2, 3 or 4 residents)
	a personal bathroom
	a shared bathroom with another room
	a locked closet/drawers
	a smoke free room
	a personal telephone

Additional Comments:

II. Resident Room - Continued

	It is Important, Somewhat important, or Not important to have...
	cable television
	the option to hang pictures
	the option to bring in furniture from home
	plants in the room
	flexible visiting hours
	flexible waking times
	flexible sleeping times
	a room near the nurses' station
	a bed next to the window
	Carpeting
	a room located on the ground floor
	in-room temperature control

Additional Comments:

III. Skilled Care/Related Skilled Services

(This group of statements pertains to the types of
skilled medical services accessible to the resident)

	It is **I**mportant, **S**omewhat important, or **N**ot important to have access to...
	personal doctor (physician name:)
	Physical therapy
	Occupational therapy
	Speech therapy
	Psychiatric services
	Podiatry services
	Optician services
	Dental services
	Hearing aid services/Audiologist
	Laboratory services
	X-ray services
	Dietician services
	Social services
	Massage therapist
	Language interpreter services (language(s):)

Additional Comments:

IV. Meals/Food Services
(This group of statements pertains to the types
of meal services accessible to the resident)

It is **I**mportant, **S**omewhat important, or **N**ot important that the nursing home meal services...	
	meet dietary needs
	meet cultural/religious needs (specify needs:)
	have option of being pre-selected
	offer choices
	are available to guests
	are available between dining hours
	are served in a dining room
	can be served in the privacy of a resident's room

Additional Comments:

V. Programs and Activities

(This group of statements pertains to the types of programs and activities accessible to the resident. Each facility varies in the type and extent of programs and activities offered.)

It is **I**mportant, **S**omewhat important, or <u>**N**</u>ot important that the following be available...	
	group activities
	individual activities
Identify activities of interest:	

Additional Comments:

VI. Miscellaneous Services

(This group of statements pertains to the miscellaneous
services supporting the nursing home)

It is **I**mportant, **S**omewhat important, or **N**ot important to have access to...	
	barber or beautician
	daily newspaper
	postal services
	in-house personal money account
	in-house worship (specify faith:)
	a public telephone
	a private place for family visits/pet visits
	a family function room
	a lounge/TV room/library
	van shuttle service for residents
	nursing home provided laundry service
	outdoor sitting areas

Additional Comments:

Next Steps:

Meet with your loved one to review and discuss your surveys. Once you understand and agree on each area, you are ready to combine worksheets #1 and #2 into worksheet #3 on pages 34-40.

Identifying Needs and Desires
Worksheet #2

*Your Name:*_____

*Date Completed:*_____

This worksheet should be completed by the individual requiring the assistance of the nursing home. Once you have made your selections, discuss your results together and reach an agreement on what you feel the needs and desires are. Use worksheet #3 on pages 34-40 to gather agreed upon results.

Each worksheet contains headings, an incomplete sentence, and a group of needs and desires. Review each section. Place an "I", an "S" or an "N" on each space in the boxes provided as the statement pertains to your needs and desires.

Use a letter **I** for important
Use a letter **S** for somewhat important
Use a letter **N** for not important

I. Facility Location
(This group of statements pertains to the
location of a desirable health care facility)

	It is **I**mportant, **S**omewhat important, or **N**ot important for the nursing home location to be...
	near family/friends
	near primary physician for easy access to appointments
	near hospital of your choice
	near preferred house of worship

Additional Comments:

I. Facility Location - Continued

	It is **I**mportant, **S**omewhat important, or **N**ot important for the nursing home location to be...
	near shopping center
	access to public transportation
	suburban (rural) location
	on busy street

Additional Comments:

II. Resident Room
(This group of statements pertains to the desirable personal room environment)

	It is Important, Somewhat important, or Not important to have...
	a private room (single occupancy)
	a semi-private room (2, 3 or 4 residents)
	a personal bathroom
	a shared bathroom with another room
	a locked closet/drawers
	a smoke free room
	a personal telephone

Additional Comments:

II. Resident Room - Continued

	It is Important, Somewhat important, or Not important to have...
	cable television
	the option to hang pictures
	the option to bring in furniture from home
	plants in the room
	flexible visiting hours
	flexible waking times
	flexible sleeping times
	a room near the nurses' station
	a bed next to the window
	Carpeting
	a room located on the ground floor
	in-room temperature control

Additional Comments:

III. Skilled Care/Related Skilled Services
(This group of statements pertains to the types of
skilled medical services accessible to the resident)

It is **I**mportant, **S**omewhat important, or **N**ot important to have access to...	
	personal doctor (physician name:)
	Physical therapy
	Occupational therapy
	Speech therapy
	Psychiatric services
	Podiatry services
	Optician services
	Dental services
	Hearing aid services/Audiologist
	Laboratory services
	X-ray services
	Dietician services
	Social services
	Massage therapist
	Language interpreter services (language(s):)

Additional Comments:

IV. Meals/Food Services
(This group of statements pertains to the types
of meal services accessible to the resident)

It is **I**mportant, **S**omewhat important, or **N**ot important
that the nursing home meal services...

	meet dietary needs
	meet cultural/religious needs (specify needs:)
	have option of being pre-selected
	offer choices
	are available to guests
	are available between dining hours
	are served in a dining room
	can be served in the privacy of a resident's room

Additional Comments:

V. Programs and Activities

(This group of statements pertains to the types of programs and
activities accessible to the resident. Each facility varies in the
type and extent of programs and activities offered.)

It is **I**mportant, **S**omewhat important, or **N**ot important that the following be available...	
	group activities
	individual activities
Identify activities of interest:	

Additional Comments:

VI. Miscellaneous Services
(This group of statements pertains to the miscellaneous
services supporting the nursing home)

	It is **I**mportant, **S**omewhat important, or **N**ot important to have access to...
	barber or beautician
	daily newspaper
	postal services
	in-house personal money account
	in-house worship (specify faith:)
	a public telephone
	a private place for family visits/pet visits
	a family function room
	a lounge/TV room/library
	van shuttle service for residents
	nursing home provided laundry service
	outdoor sitting areas

Additional Comments:

Next Steps:
Meet with your loved one to review and discuss your surveys. Once you understand and agree on each area, you are ready to combine worksheets #1 and #2 into worksheet #3 on pages 34-40.

Once worksheets #1 and #2 are completed, fill in worksheet #3. The first step in using this worksheet is to fill in the left hand side of pages 34-40 with the agreed upon responses from your individual worksheets, #1 and #2. The section with headings Nursing Home #1, #2 and #3 will be filled in later after you have visited the different facilities. This worksheet will ultimately help you compare the agreed upon needs and desires identified by yourself and your loved one with the offering of each nursing home being considered.

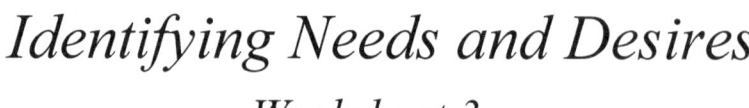

Identifying Needs and Desires
Worksheet 3

Use a letter **I** for important
Use a letter **S** for somewhat important
Use a letter **N** for not important

I. Facility Location
(This group of statements pertains to the
location of a desirable health care facility)

It is **I**mportant, **S**omewhat important, or **N**ot important for the nursing home location to be...	Nursing Home Comparisons		
	Nursing Home #1 Name:	**Nursing Home #2** Name:	**Nursing Home #3** Name:
near family/friends	Yes No	Yes No	Yes No
near primary physician	Yes No	Yes No	Yes No
near hospital of your choice	Yes No	Yes No	Yes No
near preferred house of worship	Yes No	Yes No	Yes No
near shopping center	Yes No	Yes No	Yes No
access to public transportation	Yes No	Yes No	Yes No
suburban (rural) location	Yes No	Yes No	Yes No
on busy street	Yes No	Yes No	Yes No

Additional Comments:

II. Resident Room

(This group of statements pertains to the
desirable personal room environment)

It is **I**mportant, **S**omewhat important, or **N**ot important to have...	**Nursing Home #1** Name:	**Nursing Home #2** Name:	**Nursing Home #3** Name:
a private room (single occupancy)	Yes No	Yes No	Yes No
a semi-private room (2, 3 or 4 residents)	Yes No	Yes No	Yes No
a personal bathroom	Yes No	Yes No	Yes No
a shared bathroom with another room	Yes No	Yes No	Yes No
a locked closet/drawers	Yes No	Yes No	Yes No
a smoke free room	Yes No	Yes No	Yes No
a personal telephone	Yes No	Yes No	Yes No
cable television	Yes No	Yes No	Yes No
the option to hang pictures	Yes No	Yes No	Yes No
the option to bring in furniture from home	Yes No	Yes No	Yes No
plants in the room	Yes No	Yes No	Yes No

Additional Comments:

II. Resident Room - Continued

It is Important, Somewhat important, or Not important to have...		Nursing Home #1 Name:		Nursing Home #2 Name:		Nursing Home #3 Name:	
	flexible visiting hours	Yes	No	Yes	No	Yes	No
	flexible waking times	Yes	No	Yes	No	Yes	No
	flexible sleeping times	Yes	No	Yes	No	Yes	No
	a room near the nurses' station	Yes	No	Yes	No	Yes	No
	a bed next to the window	Yes	No	Yes	No	Yes	No
	carpeting	Yes	No	Yes	No	Yes	No
	a room located on the ground floor	Yes	No	Yes	No	Yes	No
	in room temperature control	Yes	No	Yes	No	Yes	No

Additional Comments:

III. Skilled Care
(This group of statements pertains to the types of
skilled medical services accessible to the resident)

It is **I**mportant, **S**omewhat important, or **N**ot important to have access to...	Nursing Home #1 Name:		Nursing Home #2 Name:		Nursing Home #3 Name:	
personal doctor (doctor's name:)	Yes	No	Yes	No	Yes	No
Physical therapy	Yes	No	Yes	No	Yes	No
Occupational therapy	Yes	No	Yes	No	Yes	No
Speech therapy	Yes	No	Yes	No	Yes	No
Psychiatric services	Yes	No	Yes	No	Yes	No
Podiatry services	Yes	No	Yes	No	Yes	No
Optician services	Yes	No	Yes	No	Yes	No
Dental services	Yes	No	Yes	No	Yes	No
Hearing aid services/ Audiologist	Yes	No	Yes	No	Yes	No
Laboratory services	Yes	No	Yes	No	Yes	No
X-ray services	Yes	No	Yes	No	Yes	No
Dietician services	Yes	No	Yes	No	Yes	No
Social services	Yes	No	Yes	No	Yes	No
Massage therapist	Yes	No	Yes	No	Yes	No
Interpreter services (language(s):)	Yes	No	Yes	No	Yes	No

Additional Comments:

IV. Meals/Food Services

(This group of statements pertains to the types
of meal services accessible to the resident)

It is **I**mportant, **S**omewhat important, or **N**ot important that the nursing home meal services...		**Nursing Home #1** Name:		**Nursing Home #2** Name:		**Nursing Home #3** Name:	
	meet dietary needs	Yes	No	Yes	No	Yes	No
	meet cultural/religious needs (specify needs:)	Yes	No	Yes	No	Yes	No
	have option of being pre-selected	Yes	No	Yes	No	Yes	No
	offer choices	Yes	No	Yes	No	Yes	No
	are available to guests	Yes	No	Yes	No	Yes	No
	are available between dining hours	Yes	No	Yes	No	Yes	No
	are served in a dining room	Yes	No	Yes	No	Yes	No
	can be served in the privacy of a resident's room	Yes	No	Yes	No	Yes	No

Additional Comments:

V. Programs and Activities

(This group of statements pertains to the types of
programs and activities accessible to the resident.
Each facility varies in the type and extent of
programs and activities offered.)

It is **I**mportant, **S**omewhat important, or **N**ot important that the following be available...	Nursing Home #1 Name:		Nursing Home #2 Name:		Nursing Home #3 Name:	
group activities	Yes	No	Yes	No	Yes	No
individual activities	Yes	No	Yes	No	Yes	No
Identify specific activity of interest	Yes	No	Yes	No	Yes	No
Identify specific activity of interest	Yes	No	Yes	No	Yes	No
Identify specific activity of interest	Yes	No	Yes	No	Yes	No
	Yes	No	Yes	No	Yes	No
	Yes	No	Yes	No	Yes	No
	Yes	No	Yes	No	Yes	No

Additional Comments:

VI. Facility Services
(This group of statements pertains to the
miscellaneous services supporting the nursing home)

It is **I**mportant, **S**omewhat important, or **N**ot important to have access to...	Nursing Home #1 Name:		Nursing Home #2 Name:		Nursing Home #3 Name:	
barber or beautician	Yes	No	Yes	No	Yes	No
daily newspaper	Yes	No	Yes	No	Yes	No
postal services	Yes	No	Yes	No	Yes	No
in-house personal money account	Yes	No	Yes	No	Yes	No
in-house worship (specify faith:)	Yes	No	Yes	No	Yes	No
a public telephone	Yes	No	Yes	No	Yes	No
a private place for family visits/pet visits	Yes	No	Yes	No	Yes	No
a family function room	Yes	No	Yes	No	Yes	No
a lounge/TV room/library	Yes	No	Yes	No	Yes	No
van shuttle service for residents	Yes	No	Yes	No	Yes	No
nursing home laundry service	Yes	No	Yes	No	Yes	No
outdoor sitting areas	Yes	No	Yes	No	Yes	No
Additional Comments:	*Total Yes*	*Total No*	*Total Yes*	*Total No*	*Total Yes*	*Total No*

Note: Totals from pages 34-40.

Nursing Home Learning Tool

At this point, you have completed the "Identifying Needs and Desires" worksheets and have a much better idea of what to expect from a nursing home. Now is the time to begin compiling a list of the homes that you are going to visit. This is the next important step.

There are several ways to develop an initial list of nursing homes for consideration. Using the Address Log on page 44, compile a list by working with the following sources for names of potential nursing homes:

Friends or family members

Family physician or attorney

Phone book for government offices.
Contact the state Ombudsman who is familiar with area nursing homes

Yellow pages of your area phone book. In most cities, the headings are Nursing Homes, Convalescent Homes, Health Care Centers or even Rehab Centers

Town social worker for the elderly

Local library. There are national directories published with the names, addresses and phone numbers of facilities in your town, city or state.

Refer to page 93 in this guidebook for additional contacts.

Once you have identified a list of facilities that you would like to consider, use the information you have captured on the Address Log to contact each nursing home on the list. Call to introduce yourself as someone who would like to learn more about their facility. Make an appointment to meet the Admissions Coordinator or Social Service Worker. Each facility has a title for the person in charge of the admissions department.

Your first step is to begin screening each facility by telephone. Based on the "Identifying Needs and Desires" worksheets, you are now aware of some of the more important things you require from a nursing home. Prepare a set of questions to ask over the phone (identify these items on page 44, the Mandatory Screening section). These questions should be what you would consider as absolute mandatory items and without these, you might not consider that particular nursing home. Mandatory questions might include the need for a particular type of skilled care offered by the home or the availability of Medicare or Medicaid. When you make the call, pay attention to how you are received by phone. Ask yourself; "how receptive are they to my phone call and how willing are they to begin answering questions?"

Through these initial phone conversations, you may be able to narrow your list of potential facilities, hopefully to just two (2) or three (3). You do not want to spend valuable time visiting a facility only to find that they can't meet some of your mandatory needs and desires.

Once you have set meeting times with the remaining facilities on your list, you are ready to begin using the "Nursing Home Learning Tool" on pages 45-58. This tool will be your guide as you visit each facility. You have a right to know this information. In order to make an apples to apples comparison of each one you visit, use this tool so that you are comparing the same areas in each facility. Using this tool will let them know that you are knowledgeable, prepared and serious about learning what they have to offer. Before making your first visit, familiarize yourself with this learning tool. Add any thoughts or questions you may have to the tool.

The "Nursing Home Learning Tool" provides a significant amount of detail so that you can fully understand the operation of each facility. You should inquire about as many of these areas as you feel are important to you and your loved one. Before meeting with the nursing homes, go down through this list and place a check mark (✓) next to those items you definitely want to know about. Some people do not feel the need to inquire about all of these items; others feel that all are important. We have provided the detail so you can determine what is important to your selection.

You are now ready to move forward and begin learning about the nursing homes. As you go through this part of the process, keep in mind that no nursing home can replace your loved one's private home. Everyone has likes and dislikes when it comes to their home environment. Nursing homes try to provide a comfortable living environment but cannot please everyone in all areas. You are trying to find the nursing home that will be the least disruptive to your loved one's lifestyle but most of all meet the need for skilled nursing care and supervision. Keep this in mind as you begin your selection process.

Nursing Home Learning Tool

Address Log

Utilize this log to keep track of the nursing
homes you wish to make initial contact with.

Nursing Home Name	Phone Number	Address	Contact Name	Appointment Date

Prepare a set of preliminary questions to ask the initial nursing homes that you contact. These questions should be mandatory items that you or your loved one require from a nursing home and will serve in your initial screening.

Mandatory screening questions to ask before you visit a nursing home:

_____

_____

_____

_____

_____

Nursing Home Learning Tool

This worksheet should be filled in as you visit each nursing home. To make comparisons of the facilities easier, circle the corresponding "Yes" or "No" as it relates to each area.

	#1	**#2**	**#3**
Facility Name:			
Address:			
Phone:			
Contact:			

Note:

Sections **A.**, **B.**, and **C.** are perhaps the most important of this tool. If you feel uncomfortable with any of the responses from a particular facility, it may be cause for concern and may need further discussion with representatives from the particular facility.

A. Licensure

	#1	**#2**	**#3**
current license	Yes No	Yes No	Yes No
current Administrator's license	Yes No	Yes No	Yes No
JCAHO accreditation See definition - pg. 90	Yes No	Yes No	Yes No
Free of State violations: (call State Health Dept.)	Yes No	Yes No	Yes No
Free of Federal violations: (call State Health Dept.)	Yes No	Yes No	Yes No

B. Financial Programs

	#1	#2	#3
Medicare certified	Yes No	Yes No	Yes No
Medicaid certified	Yes No	Yes No	Yes No

C. Residents' Appearance

	#1	#2	#3
residents are clean in appearance	Yes No	Yes No	Yes No
residents observed are odor free	Yes No	Yes No	Yes No
residents' demeanor is happy	Yes No	Yes No	Yes No
residents socialize with ease	Yes No	Yes No	Yes No
residents are involved/ occupied in activity	Yes No	Yes No	Yes No

I. Facility Location #1

✓		#1		#2		#3	
	near family/friends	Yes	No	Yes	No	Yes	No
	near primary physician (for easy access to appointments) Physician:	Yes	No	Yes	No	Yes	No
	near hospital of your choice Hospital:	Yes	No	Yes	No	Yes	No
	near preferred house of worship	Yes	No	Yes	No	Yes	No
	near shopping center	Yes	No	Yes	No	Yes	No
	access to public transportation	Yes	No	Yes	No	Yes	No
	suburban (rural) location	Yes	No	Yes	No	Yes	No
	on busy street	Yes	No	Yes	No	Yes	No

II. Resident Room #1

✓		#1		#2		#3	
	Patient Bill of Rights posted (may be posted elsewhere)	Yes	No	Yes	No	Yes	No
	complaint/grievance policy posted	Yes	No	Yes	No	Yes	No
	private room available private bathroom	Yes Yes	No No	Yes Yes	No No	Yes Yes	No No
	semi-private room (2 persons) avail. in room bathroom	Yes Yes	No No	Yes Yes	No No	Yes Yes	No No
	semi-private room (3 persons) avail. in room bathroom	Yes Yes	No No	Yes Yes	No No	Yes Yes	No No

II. Resident Room - Continued

✓		#1		#2		#3	
	semi-private room (4 persons) avail. in room bathroom	Yes Yes	No No	Yes Yes	No No	Yes Yes	No No
	choice of room choice of side of room	Yes Yes	No No	Yes Yes	No No	Yes Yes	No No
	available closet space	Yes	No	Yes	No	Yes	No
	ability to lock closet/drawers	Yes	No	Yes	No	Yes	No
	smoking allowed in room	Yes	No	Yes	No	Yes	No
	telephone installation allowed	Yes	No	Yes	No	Yes	No
	cable television installation allowed	Yes	No	Yes	No	Yes	No
	ability to hang personal pictures	Yes	No	Yes	No	Yes	No
	furniture allowed from home what kind	Yes	No	Yes	No	Yes	No
	ability to have plants	Yes	No	Yes	No	Yes	No
	accommodates any bed time/ nap time	Yes	No	Yes	No	Yes	No
	accommodates early morning risers	Yes	No	Yes	No	Yes	No
	light switches easy to reach (especially from wheelchair)	Yes	No	Yes	No	Yes	No
	door handles easy to use	Yes	No	Yes	No	Yes	No
	Nurses call bell within reach of bed/chair	Yes	No	Yes	No	Yes	No

II. Resident Room - Continued

✓		#1	#2	#3
	safety bed rails functioning (test these yourself)	Yes No	Yes No	Yes No
	bed, chair, night stand supplied by facility	Yes No	Yes No	Yes No
	bathroom well lighted	Yes No	Yes No	Yes No
	bathroom has handrails	Yes No	Yes No	Yes No
	bathroom door opens both ways (should operate both ways)	Yes No	Yes No	Yes No
	ease of wheelchairs/walking devices on flooring	Yes No	Yes No	Yes No
	windows able to be opened if open: safety measures	Yes No	Yes No	Yes No . . . .
	room lighting appropriate	Yes No	Yes No	Yes No

III. Related Skilled Services #1

✓		#1	#2	#3
	Medical Director is a physician	Yes No	Yes No	Yes No
	monthly resident evaluation is made by Medical Director	Yes No	Yes No	Yes No
	physicians review their orders monthly	Yes No	Yes No	Yes No
	personal doctor works with facility name	Yes No	Yes No	Yes No . . . .

III. Related Skilled Services - Continued

✓		#1		#2		#3	
	Physical Therapist provided by facility	Yes	No	Yes	No	Yes	No
	Occupational Therapist provided by facility	Yes	No	Yes	No	Yes	No
	Speech Therapist provided by facility	Yes	No	Yes	No	Yes	No
	Psychiatric services provided by facility	Yes	No	Yes	No	Yes	No
	Podiatry services provided by facility	Yes	No	Yes	No	Yes	No
	Optician services provided by facility	Yes	No	Yes	No	Yes	No
	Dental services provided by facility	Yes	No	Yes	No	Yes	No
	Hearing aid services/audiology provided by facility	Yes	No	Yes	No	Yes	No
	Laboratory services provided by facility	Yes	No	Yes	No	Yes	No
	X-ray services provided by facility	Yes	No	Yes	No	Yes	No
	Dietician services provided by facility	Yes	No	Yes	No	Yes	No
	Social services provided by facility	Yes	No	Yes	No	Yes	No

III. Related Skilled Services - Continued

✓		#1	#2	#3
	Massage therapist provided by facility	Yes No	Yes No	Yes No
	Language interpreter services provided by facility language(s)	. . . .	. . . .	. . . .

IV. Food Services

✓		#1	#2	#3
	meals meet individual dietary needs	Yes No	Yes No	Yes No
	cultural/religious diversity considered	Yes No	Yes No	Yes No
	meals pre-selected	Yes No	Yes No	Yes No
	meal choices offered	Yes No	Yes No	Yes No
	meals available to guests	Yes No	Yes No	Yes No
	meals available between dining hours	Yes No	Yes No	Yes No
	meals served in dining room	Yes No	Yes No	Yes No
	dining room well lighted	Yes No	Yes No	Yes No
	meals served in privacy of resident's room	Yes No	Yes No	Yes No
	snacks offered	Yes No	Yes No	Yes No
	meals posted	Yes No	Yes No	Yes No

V. Programs and Activities

✓		#1		#2		#3	
	group activities available	Yes	No	Yes	No	Yes	No
	individual activities available	Yes	No	Yes	No	Yes	No
	activities posted in plain view frequency of activities . . . . . . frequency of outings	Yes	No	Yes	No	Yes	No
	voting capabilities	Yes	No	Yes	No	Yes	No
	meets your loved one's activity/ hobby desire	Yes	No	Yes	No	Yes	No

VI. Miscellaneous Services

✓		#1		#2		#3	
	access to barber/beautician	Yes	No	Yes	No	Yes	No
	access to newspaper delivery	Yes	No	Yes	No	Yes	No
	access to postal services	Yes	No	Yes	No	Yes	No
	access to personal in-house money account	Yes	No	Yes	No	Yes	No
	in-house worship area	Yes	No	Yes	No	Yes	No
	access to public telephone	Yes	No	Yes	No	Yes	No
	a private place for family visits/ pet visits	Yes	No	Yes	No	Yes	No
	access to family function room	Yes	No	Yes	No	Yes	No

VI. Miscellaneous Services - Continued

✓		#1		#2		#3	
	access to lounge/TV facilities	Yes	No	Yes	No	Yes	No
	access to van shuttle service	Yes	No	Yes	No	Yes	No

VII. Facility's Physical Considerations

✓		#1		#2		#3	
	1 story building	Yes	No	Yes	No	Yes	No
	multiple story building	Yes	No	Yes	No	Yes	No
	ease of elevator access and use (if applicable)	Yes	No	Yes	No	Yes	No
	general appearance clean outside	Yes	No	Yes	No	Yes	No
	general appearance clean inside	Yes	No	Yes	No	Yes	No
	exit signs clearly marked	Yes	No	Yes	No	Yes	No
	exits free of obstructions	Yes	No	Yes	No	Yes	No
	emergency exit plans visible on each unit	Yes	No	Yes	No	Yes	No
	areas used by residents well lighted	Yes	No	Yes	No	Yes	No
	corridors have handrails on both sides	Yes	No	Yes	No	Yes	No
	access to shower	Yes	No	Yes	No	Yes	No
	wheelchair accessible shower	Yes	No	Yes	No	Yes	No

VII. Facility's Physical Considerations - Continued

✓		#1		#2		#3	
	access to tub	Yes	No	Yes	No	Yes	No
	wheelchair accessible to tub	Yes	No	Yes	No	Yes	No
	hand rails/grab bars in shower	Yes	No	Yes	No	Yes	No
	hand rails/grab bars in tub	Yes	No	Yes	No	Yes	No
	building exterior well lighted	Yes	No	Yes	No	Yes	No
	ease of resident pick up and dropoff	Yes	No	Yes	No	Yes	No
	ease of resident access to outdoors	Yes	No	Yes	No	Yes	No
	easy visitor access to building	Yes	No	Yes	No	Yes	No
	convenient visitor parking	Yes	No	Yes	No	Yes	No

VIII. Skilled Nursing Care

✓		#1	#2	#3
	number of residents per unit			
	number of nurses (per resident) 7a.m.-3p.m. shift . . . . 3p.m.-11p.m. shift . . . . 11p.m.-7a.m. shift	Yes No	Yes No	Yes No . . . .
	number of nurses aides (per resident) 7a.m.-3p.m. shift . . . . 3p.m.-11p.m. shift . . . . 11p.m.-7a.m. shift	Yes No	Yes No	Yes No . . . .
	nursing staff is organized through a union	Yes No	Yes No	Yes No
	each unit has a primary care nurse	Yes No	Yes No	Yes No
	primary care nurse responsible for plan of care If no: who is responsible . . .	Yes No	Yes No	Yes No . . . .
	resident plan of care frequently reviewed frequency of plan evaluation.	Yes No	Yes No	Yes No . . . .
	medications administered by nurses	Yes No	Yes No	Yes No
	nurses aides supervised by nurse	Yes No	Yes No	Yes No
	procedure for bedridden resident care	Yes No	Yes No	Yes No
	toileting procedure followed	Yes No	Yes No	Yes No
	toileting before meals	Yes No	Yes No	Yes No
	no toileting during meals	Yes No	Yes No	Yes No
	bathing procedure	Yes No	Yes No	Yes No

IX. Facility Emergency Plan

✓		#1		#2		#3	
	emergency plan manual on each unit	Yes	No	Yes	No	Yes	No
	emergency drills rehearsed frequently	Yes	No	Yes	No	Yes	No

X. Housekeeping and Laundry

✓		#1		#2		#3	
	maintenance equipment safely out of reach of residents	Yes	No	Yes	No	Yes	No
	facility clean in appearance	Yes	No	Yes	No	Yes	No
	personal laundry by facility fee:	Yes	No	Yes	No	Yes	No . . . .
	personal laundry returned within 5-7 days	Yes	No	Yes	No	Yes	No
	consideration given for laundry allergies	Yes	No	Yes	No	Yes	No
	generally clean appearance of bed linens	Yes	No	Yes	No	Yes	No
	fresh linen carts covered	Yes	No	Yes	No	Yes	No
	clean and soiled linen carts covered	Yes	No	Yes	No	Yes	No

XI. Cost Information

	#1	#2	#3
Cost for Private Room			
Per day	. . . .	. . . .	. . . .
Per month	. . . .	. . . .	. . . .
Per year	. . . .	. . . .	. . . .
Payer source reimbursement amount	. . . .	. . . .	. . . .
Cost for Semi-Private Room (2 people)			
Per day	. . . .	. . . .	. . . .
Per month	. . . .	. . . .	. . . .
Per year	. . . .	. . . .	. . . .
Payer source reimbursement amount	. . . .	. . . .	. . . .
Cost for Semi-Private Room (3 people)			
Per day	. . . .	. . . .	. . . .
Per month	. . . .	. . . .	. . . .
Per year	. . . .	. . . .	. . . .
Payer source reimbursement amount	. . . .	. . . .	. . . .
Cost for Semi-Private Room (4 people)			
Per day	. . . .	. . . .	. . . .
Per month	. . . .	. . . .	. . . .
Per year	. . . .	. . . .	. . . .
Payer source reimbursement amount	. . . .	. . . .	. . . .

XIV. Cost Information - Continued

	#1	#2	#3
down payment required if yes, amount required	Yes No	Yes No	Yes No . . . .
billing schedule			
processing fees/one time charges			
approximate time of wait for admission			
procedures for annual price increases			
payment methods accepted			

Making The Decision

Congratulations, you have completed the most time consuming part of the nursing home search and perhaps have even made your selection. If not, you are ready to evaluate the information you have collected to decide on a facility that meets your loved one's needs. As each person has different needs, desires, questions and concerns, so too is their decision making process. Therefore, the decision can not be made into a clear black and white process. The worksheets available in this guide are offered to help you organize the process and to identify items that may or may not be important to you.

In going through this process, you most likely have already developed a confidence in a particular nursing home. If it is apparent to you which facility is best suited for your loved one, then proceed to page 61, "Preparing for the Transition". In the event you have not developed a confidence in a particular nursing home that you have already learned about, you may want to follow the procedure below. This procedure is designed to assist you in further organizing the information you have gathered and may help you to make a decision. Keep in mind that you may want to broaden your search to additional nursing homes if you have not developed a confidence in a particular one.

Proceed with the following steps if you have not developed a confidence in a particular nursing home:

Step 1: Evaluate the "No" responses on the "Nursing Home Learning Tool" for each facility. With your loved one, consider the importance of the "No" responses.

Step 2: Return to worksheet #3 titled "Identifying Needs and Desires" on pages 34-40 to compare the information you have collected on each facility with the   identified needs and desires on the worksheet.

Step 3: Draw a circle around the "Yes" if the facility has the ability to satisfy the "important" (I) and "somewhat important" (S) items you have chosen under facility location, resident room, skilled care, meals/food services, programs and activities, and facility services. Draw a circle around the "No" if the facility cannot satisfy the important items you have chosen.

Step 4: Once you have completed this process, examine the number of "important" (I) and "somewhat important"(S) items that can be satisfied by each facility to the number of items that are "important" (I) and "somewhat important" (S) that cannot be satisfied.

Step 5: Determine if the items that are "important" (I) and "somewhat important" (S) and cannot be satisfied by a particular facility are in fact a priority to your loved one.

Step 6: In the box at the end of Worksheet #3 on page 40, place the number of circled "Yes" and "No" responses you count for each facility as related to the "important" (I) and "somewhat important" (S) items. Once you have filled in each box you will be able to see which facility has the ability to meet the majority of your loved one's needs and desires.

Preparing For The Transition

By the time you've reached this point, a nursing home has been selected. You've taken the time and did the preparation to make an informed decision. This, however, is not the end.

Emotional and Logistical Preparation

Too many people feel that once a nursing home is selected, the process is complete. Although the selection process is critical, so too is making the transition. It's at this point that you can help ease the emotional and logistical issues in moving your loved one from the home into a nursing home facility. Being aware of the preparatory steps that should be taken at this time will help ensure an easier transition for all involved. The nursing home you have selected will be able to help your loved one, yourself and other family members through the transition. Ask the social worker and nurse at the nursing home for assistance during this important time.

Coping with Emotions

First, all family members involved need to be sensitive to the transition that will be taking place. One of life's great pleasures is living independently and doing so with dignity. Having to give up living independence can create a wide spectrum of emotions. These emotions can be strongest at the time of making final move preparations. This is not the time for any family member to deny the existence of their heightened emotions. To deny the presence of emotional strains at this time is not healthy. It is important to share and communicate your emotions with loved ones. Doing so will reduce anxieties and create dialogue that can help ease the emotional transition. For all family members involved it is important to keep this in mind.

Take the opportunity to ask yourself, your loved one and other family members questions that will open a healthy dialogue. Provide an environment that encourages expression of emotions -

How and what are you feeling?
What are close family members feeling?
How will your lives change or be impacted by these
   decisions?

Communicating the Positive

One of the most common feelings during this time for family members is one of guilt. Family members involved in making this decision need to be prepared for the guilt that they will experience throughout this entire time. We love our parents, grandparents, aunts and uncles and would like to care for them ourselves. This is not always practical whether it be for medical or social reasons. It is very important during this time of transition to acknowledge the many feelings being experienced and to reinforce the following:

Decision was thought through and carefully made.
Better daily care can now be provided to your loved one.
More friends and activities will be available than could
   be provided at home.
Your loved one will continue to be important to everyone
   in the family.

Logistical Preparations

In addition to the emotional considerations that need to be made, there are logistical ones as well. This time of transition can also be eased by making advanced preparations. This preparation comes in several forms:

Phone Log - The nursing home that your loved one is moving to has many points of contact. It will be helpful to utilize the phone log provided on page 65. Use this log to keep track of the important phone numbers of key personnel and departments within the nursing home. This log should be readily available to a family member who will be staying in contact with the facility.

Personal Inventory - Whether it be an article of clothing or a personal item, such as a picture, there should be a record maintained as to what has been brought to the nursing home. Use pages 66 and 67 to a keep personal inventory list.

Case Journal - Another logistical tool provided to ease the transition is the Case Journal. On a periodic basis, you or another family member will be meeting with representatives of the nursing home staff to discuss the care of your loved one. These meetings are very important and a record of them should be maintained. Utilize the Case Journals on pages 68 and 69 to keep track of items discussed and to follow up on actions that are planned.

Transition Checklist - To help you keep track of the preparation steps, utilize the checklist on pages 70 and 71 to make sure you don't forget important items.

Resident Introduction - Although most nursing homes will take important information pertaining to your loved one prior to the first day, not all of them will ask specifically about personal likes and dislikes. Utilize the form on page 72 to provide important personal information to help the nursing home better understand your loved one.

Love is Most Important

Emotional and logistical preparation is the key to a smooth transition for all. Always remember that a nursing home does not replace family or friends. A nursing home provides a valuable service in the community that brings with it the benefits of skilled nursing care, new friends and new activities. The experience in the nursing home will be benefited by continued strong contact with outside family and friends. One way to have continued contact is to develop a visiting schedule with other family members and friends. The schedule can be organized around work and family commitments. If distance is a problem, try to find someone locally that can provide regular visits. Love is the most needed of all human needs to be satisfied at this time. If you remember nothing else during the transition, remember the importance of love.

Phone Log

It is important that you keep a record of the phone numbers for key personnel at the nursing home you have selected. Utilize this log as an easy reference tool.

Facility Name:_____

Address:_____

City, State, Zip:_____

Main Phone #:_____

Position Title	Name	Phone Number
Facility Administrator		
Director of Nursing		
Ass't Director of Nursing		
Medical Director		
Nurses		
Other Medical Staff		
Social Service Director		
Recreation Director		
Other Staff		
Resident's Phone		

Personal Inventory List

Date: _____

Undergarments:
- undershirts_____
- underpants_____
- bras_____
- other_____

Sweaters:
- cardigan_____
- pullover_____
- vest_____

Shirts:
- button down_____
- long sleeve_____
- short sleeve_____
- pullover_____
- tank tops_____
- turtle necks_____
- blouses_____
- long sleeve_____
- short sleeve_____
- other_____

Pants:
- dress slacks_____
- casual_____
- pant suits_____
- man's suit_____
- sweat pants_____
- sweat suit set_____
- shorts_____
- short sets_____
- jeans_____

Night Wear:
- pajama set_____
- top_____
- bottoms_____
- night gown_____
- slippers_____(pairs)
- other_____

Skirts:
- dress_____
- casual_____
- Ssorts_____

Dresses:
- dressy_____
- casual_____
- lady's skirt suits_____

Shoes: (pairs)
- dress_____
- casual_____
- sneakers_____
- sandals_____
- boots_____
- orthopedic_____
- other_____

Socks: (pairs)
- dress_____
- casual_____
- nylons_____
- knee highs_____
- trouser socks_____

Jackets:
- formal_____
- casual_____
- blazers_____
- spring_____
- fall_____
- winter_____
- other_____

Accessories:
- belts_____
- suspenders_____
- ties_____
- gloves_____
- scarves_____
- Winter_____
- dress_____
- rings_____
- necklaces_____
- earrings_____
- watch_____
- jewelry case_____
- brooches_____
- cuff links_____
- tie clip_____
- purse(s)_____
- hat(s)_____
- other_____
- other_____
- other_____
- other_____

Linens:

afghan(s) _____
  color _____
blanket(s) _____
  color _____
Quilt _____
  color _____
pillow(s) _____
  cases _____
  color _____
luggage _____
  style _____
  color _____

Room Furnishings:

chair _____
  style _____
  color _____
  cushions _____
    color _____
lamp(s) _____
  table lamp _____
  floor lamp _____
table(s) _____
  bedside _____
  television _____
  end table _____
  plant table _____
bureau _____
foot stool _____
  color _____
other _____
other _____
other _____

Room Accessories:

clock _____
  brand name _____
  style _____
  describe _____
radio _____
  brand name _____
  serial # _____
walkman radio/
cassette player _____
  brand name _____
  serial # _____
television _____
  brand name _____
  serial # _____
  remote: Yes No
VCR _____
  brand name _____
  serial # _____
  remote: Yes No
telephone _____
  brand name _____
  color _____
answering machine ___
  brand name _____
  serial # _____
room fan _____
  name brand _____
  serial # _____

Room Decorations:

pictures _____
flower vases _____
other _____

Other:

calculator _____
camera _____
  brand name _____
  serial # _____
  case _____
  color _____
photo album(s) _____

Durable Medical Equipment:

cane _____
  three point cane _____
  quad cane _____
crutch(es) _____
walker _____
brace(s) _____
wheelchair _____
bedside commode _____
other _____

Personal Medical Items:

hearing aid _____
  right ear _____
  left ear _____
  case _____
dentures _____
  upper _____
  lower _____
  partial _____
glasses _____
  bifocals _____
  sunglasses _____
other _____

Case Conference Journal

On a periodic basis, you'll be meeting with representatives of the nursing home. Utilize this journal to keep a record of the meetings and the points discussed.

Prepared For: _____

Date: _____

Attendees: _____   _____

_____   _____

_____   _____

_____   _____

Discussion Points: _____

_____

_____

_____

_____

_____

_____

Plan: _____

_____

_____

_____

_____

_____

Case Conference Journal

On a periodic basis, you'll be meeting with representatives of the nursing home. Utilize this journal to keep a record of the meetings and the points discussed.

Prepared For: _____

Date: _____

Attendees: _____   _____

_____   _____

_____   _____

_____   _____

Discussion Points: _____

_____

_____

_____

_____

_____

Plan: _____

_____

_____

_____

_____

Transition Checklist

Items to do for a Smoother Transition

		Completed	**Remarks**
Change of address cards to Post Office			
Change of address cards to family/friends			
Change of address notification to:			
(List)	Magazines		
	#1		
	#2		
	#3		
(List)	Newspaper		
	#1		
	#2		
(List)	Credit Cards		
	#1		
	#2		
	#3		
(List)	Memberships/Organization Affiliations		
	#1		
	#2		
	#3		
Phone Hook Up			
Cable TV Hook Up			

	Completed	Remarks
Prepare Clothing		
Label items		
Complete Inventory Checklist		
Prepare Personal Items		
Label items		
Complete Inventory Checklist		
Miscellaneous		

Resident Introduction

Date:_____ **Nursing Home:**_____

Resident Full Name: _____
             (First)   *(Last)*   *(Initial)*

☐ **Smoker**   ☐ **Non Smoker**   **Allergies:**_____

Preferred Meal Times:

Breakfast_____AM

Lunch_____PM

Dinner_____PM

Snack times_____

__ _____

__ _____

__ _____

Food Likes and Dislikes:

Likes:_____

_____

Dislikes:_____

_____

Diet Restrictions:_____

_____

Preferred Times For:

Evening Sleeping_____AM   Morning Waking_____PM

Nap_____AM/PM   Nap_____AM/PM

Activities/Hobbies of Interest:

_____

_____

_____

Religious Worship:_____

Commonly Asked Questions

Q. We're not sure how we're going to pay for a nursing home. What are our options?

A. This is a difficult question that faces every individual and family that is considering a nursing home. The only options available are; personal resources, private insurance, Medicaid or Medicare. Each of these will depend on your particular financial situation. To determine the best method, discuss this with an estate planner or elder law attorney. In the event none of these are available to you, contact your local social worker or local office of the American Association of Retired Persons for guidance.

Q. I'm not sure my mother needs an updated Will or an Estate Plan. Do we need to consider these things now?

A. As part of the overall question of finances, this question also should be addressed. Depending on your personal financial situation, you may require the assistance of an attorney that specializes in wills and estate planning. In actuality, this question should be addressed as early on as possible, even prior to the need for a nursing home.

Q. Should we be considering a Living Will for my uncle?

A. A Living Will, or Advanced Directive, gives specific health care directions in the event an individual cannot speak for him or herself. It is recommended to have one drawn up. Consult with your attorney or local social worker regarding the procedure in your area for obtaining a Living Will. Another approach is to contact your State Department of Health to find out if they have information. A fee for a Living Will can be limited to a notary public or an attorney.

Q. I believe my mother needs the skilled care of a nursing home but my brother feels she should be at home. What should we do?

A. This is a common situation facing many families. If you find that by yourselves you cannot come to agreement, then outside counseling is necessary. The question that needs to be answered is: does your mother need professional skilled care that is only available through a nursing home or can her needs be met at home? There are several places you can turn including your mother's doctor for an assessment of what daily medical care needs exist. In the event this is not the deciding factor, other close individuals to your family can provide input and guidance such as: clergy, family attorney or local social worker.

Q. My father is currently in a nursing home but hates it. Should I look to move him to another one or will it just be the same?

A. You should first determine what it is your father dislikes. Is it the particular home or just the overall concept of nursing homes? See if your father can give you specifics and address these with the nurse. If there are particular issues that are not or cannot be addressed by the nursing home, then it is time to evaluate a more suitable home. Often times, families select a nursing home under pressure. They find out later that the home they first thought would be appropriate did not meet all their needs. Don't be afraid to find another facility based on the experience you've gained. Once you have found a new home for your father, notify the present facility. Allow them time to prepare the appropriate documents for your father's transfer, such as medical history, medications and other pertinent information. This process may take a day or more. Be sure to consult with the present facility's billing department regarding any outstanding charges. You should be aware of any prorated charges. It would be unfortunate to remove your father a day or two earlier than policy states and have to pay for a room your father is no longer using.

Q. Is it normal to feel guilty while going through this process? I love my mother but I need some help taking care of her.

A. Guilt is the most common emotion felt by family members at this time. We feel guilty because our parents took care of us while we were growing up that we should return the care. This may be true for some, but for others it is difficult because they have to care for their own family. You need to feel confident that you are selecting a nursing home because it is the environment in which your mother will receive the proper professional care that you are unable to provide at home.

Q. How much time should I allocate to find the right nursing home? Is a week or two realistic?

A. There is no specific rule to go by. Some people take a few weeks and make a great decision. Others take months only to feel uncomfortable with their decision. It's not so much the time as it is the process you go through. The phrase "work smart, not hard" certainly applies here. Organize and plan your approach using a guidebook, such as this one, to help you utilize the time you do have effectively.

Q. What clothing should we provide for our mother?

A. Provide clothes that are the most comfortable and suitable to your mother's personal style and needs. Purchasing new clothes is not necessary unless you feel the need to replace undesirable clothing. You may want to consider the temperature of her new room, surroundings, and outdoors to determine what clothing is appropriate. Try to bring the clothing that your mother wears on a day-to-day basis. Remember, this will be her home. Make her as comfortable as you can.

Q. How much clothing should we pack for her?

A. Before entering the facility, decide how laundry needs will be handled - by the laundry department or by family or friends. This decision will help you in deciding how much clothing to pack. Be sure to bring enough to last for seven (7) to ten (10) days. The average time for clothes to return from the laundry department of most facilities is five (5) to seven (7) days. The time of return will vary depending on each facility's laundry department capabilities and the staff managing the department. Ask the laundry supervisor about their average turn around time. Also ask the laundry supervisor if there is an assigned person to manage laundering of personal clothes or if all laundry personnel handle personal clothes and house linens. The answer will help you decide who will handle the laundry needs. Be sure to inform the nurse and the laundry supervisor of any detergent allergies your mother may have. This information is important for the staff to properly manage her laundry if you choose the facility to care for this need.

Q. My grandmother's doctor is recommending she move into a nursing home. I don't like this option and am delaying looking for a facility. What should I do if I think her doctor is wrong?

A. Your first step is to talk it through with your grandmother. If she is not capable of helping in the decision then you should talk openly with the doctor. Give him/her an opportunity to clearly layout the reasons for suggesting the nursing home. If you still cannot agree, then it's time for another doctor's opinion. If the reason is not purely medical in nature, obtain outside input from other family members, clergy, family attorney, a social worker or nurse practitioner.

Q. How will the staff know which personal clothing is my father's?

A. To ensure the staff knows which clothing is his, you should label each article before packing it for him. There are two ways to label the clothing. You can use permanent markers or you can sew in personalized labels. Either way, be sure that your father's name is legibly written on all clothing including: socks, undergarments, belts, suspenders, and the inside of shoes. Put the last name first then the first name; this will help eliminate confusion if another resident bears the same last name. It is not necessary to put his room number on clothing, unless it is the facility's policy. Putting the room number on his clothing can create a problem for him if he decides to relocate to another room at a future time. Many people choose to sew a personalized label in their clothing. Check with a local fabric store for availability of labels; most have to be ordered in advance. Be sure to ask the store clerk if you can see a sample of the label. Some labels are made of rough fabric which can irritate or harm fragile skin. Labels should be placed on clothing where they will have the least contact with skin in order to avoid irritation.

Q. What kind of shoes should my grandmother bring to wear?

A. A physical therapy evaluation should be performed in a timely manner upon arriving for her first day. The therapist will recommend the appropriate shoes for the environment. Rubber soled shoes are highly recommended if the environment consists of linoleum or other smooth flooring surfaces. Be sure to inform the physical therapist of her preferred footwear or the footwear that she is accustomed to wearing. This information will help the therapist make a better decision on appropriate footwear.

Q. My father has favorite pictures. Can he bring them?

A. Pictures are encouraged to make the environment his own. Most maintenance departments within facilities will assist you in hanging any personal items on walls. Pictures that stand upright on a table are also acceptable. Be sure to put his name on the back, as well as other personal items he may be bringing with him.

Q. Can my aunt bring her favorite chair?

A. It is important to have items from home that will make her new home comfortable. Be sure to consult with the Social Service Department concerning the amount and size of furniture she can bring in. Most rooms have space available to use. The amount of space available differs from room to room. Also consider the safety of items. For example, the age of lamp wires should be inspected for safety before using it in the new room. If you are uncertain about the safety of an electrical item, ask the maintenance department to thoroughly evaluate it and label it for safety. Other items, such as the bed from her home, are not suitable for the facility. The bed that is available in the new environment is a requirement of the facility. She is welcome to bring in a bed cover and pillow that fits her new bed. Lastly, throw rugs are not appropriate to bring into her new room. These types of rugs are a safety hazard for your aunt and the staff as the rugs are not secured to the floor creating the potential of slipping. As mentioned earlier, be sure to label those items brought with her.

When in doubt about the safety or appropriateness of an item in her new environment, be sure to ask the nurse or a member of the Social Service Department. Both are familiar with the facility's rules and regulations.

Q. What personal hygiene products can my mother bring? What does the facility supply?

A. Personal hygiene products are just that ... personal. Most people have a favorite brand name product that they choose to use. If you can purchase the products she prefers then that is best. Be sure to review with her nurse which products are acceptable to use in the facility. Label each item with a permanent marker with her last name and first name to ensure that the item will remain in her possession and not be misplaced. It would be helpful to your mother and the staff to have a personalized container to store and carry her personal hygiene products. Label the container as you have labelled her other items. Many facilities supply personal items such as toothpaste, toothbrushes, combs, hairbrushes, shampoo, soap, sanitary napkins, and razors. These products may not be the same brand that she prefers to use. Discuss with your mother's nurse what items the facility offers and decide what is appropriate for her to use. Remember to consider your means of purchasing products that she prefers. It is not the facility's responsibility to obtain commercially sold products for her use. Be sure to inform your mother's nurse of any allergies your mother may have to any over-the-counter products.

Q. My mother doesn't want to be without her favorite jewelry. What can she bring?

A. We all have jewelry that we value. The idea of leaving these behind can be painful. It is important to realize that there is a chance that the item(s) we hold so dear to us can easily be lost. It is not recommended that jewelry be in your mother's room unless it can be worn by her at all times comfortably and not inhibit her abilities or interfere with her plan of care. Remember that certain jewelry pieces are not safe to wear during certain activities. As an example, a long necklace worn during sleep can become tangled in the bed linens and cause serious injury. Even wearing earrings to bed can cause injury to ear lobes. Additionally, determine if the closets or drawers in your mother's room allow her to lock away valuables with a key that can be kept with her at all times. If the facility does not have these capabilities or provide a central vault or safe, you must consider which pieces are safe for her to bring and are appropriate for all of her activities. Err on the side of safety so she doesn't harm herself, harm others, or even worse, lose that precious piece that means so much to her.

Q. Do we need to make sure our father has cash with him?

A. It is not necessary for your father to have a large sum of money with him. The facility you have chosen may offer a store which can consist of a small variety of personal items, magazines, gifts, or stationery. Some even offer food items. If he desires to have a newspaper, you can arrange with the facility's Social Service Department or office staff to have it delivered, if this service is available. Keep in mind that you or your father is responsible for paying for the newspaper, the facility may not supply one for each resident. Also check with the office staff about opening a personal money account from which the newspaper can be deducted or even for the fee for the barber/beautician. The account should be accessible by your father and another family member during office hours. Be sure to check with the office staff frequently regarding the status of the account.

Q. I'd like my uncle to have his television. Is that allowed?

A. Many people find watching television an entertaining activity. Most facilities allow each resident to put a television in the room. Before bringing in a television, look around the room and determine the safest place for it. Keep in mind that it should be placed on a strong sturdy surface that can hold the weight. Remember to err on the side of safety. In addition, do not provide an older television that has frayed wires. If you are concerned about the safety of the television's electrical capabilities or the sturdiness of the surface it is resting on, ask the facility's maintenance department for help. The television should not obstruct a major walkway or obstruct wheelchair access to any side of the room. A console or floor unit television is not appropriate to have. Place the television so that your uncle can adequately view the screen from several sitting positions in his room. You may need to be sensitive to cable television outlets as well. A television with a remote control with few controls that are large and easy to see and press is the best type of remote for individuals who have difficulty handling fine objects or have declining vision. Remind your uncle to be considerate of his roommate(s) if he resides in a semi-private room. Imagine yourself in a room with someone whose television is disruptive to you. The volume should be controlled so that only your uncle can hear the program he is watching, unless his roommate is viewing as well. The sleeping and napping patterns of his roommate should be taken into consideration. You may even consider providing head phones to eliminate the noise issue. Consideration in this fashion can maintain a positive relationship with others. If his roommate discourages his viewing the television, your best approach is to speak with the nurse and the Social Service Department about the options. You may also want to consider discussing the issue with the roommate to determine the exact time your uncle can enjoy his favorite programs without being disturbed and without disturbing his roommate.

Q. Can my father have cable television in his room?

A. Cable television is a luxury most of us enjoy. Many of us have a favorite program that can only be viewed on a cable channel. Not all facilities supply cable television for the residents in their room. Cable television may be available in designated areas of the facility such as the recreation room or the lounges. Be prepared to pay for cable television installation in his room and for the monthly charges from the cable company if the facility allows the hookup. Before entering the facility for the very first day, consult with the nurse or Social Service Department about the procedure for purchasing cable television.

Q. My mother likes to talk to family and friends on the phone, can she have a phone in her room?

A. Communicating with family and friends is an important part of our daily lives. Without contact with them we can feel alone and isolated. Each facility should have a telephone jack to accept her telephone. Again, be prepared to pay for the telephone company's installation, monthly, and long-distance fees. It is not the responsibility of the facility to supply a telephone or telephone service to each resident's room. Remind your mother to be considerate of those around her while using the telephone. Keep the wires out of walkways and wheelchair access ways. Your mother and others can trip on the wire and sustain an injury while damaging the telephone. Place the telephone within reach from her bed and the place she sits in the room. A public telephone that accepts coins for operation should be available and accessible for her to use as well.

Q. I just refilled prescriptions, can my father bring them with him?

A. On the first day in the nursing home, the nurse will perform a complete evaluation of your father and his medical care as part of admission to the facility. Bring the medications so the nurse can examine each bottle and consult with the physician regarding medication orders. If you have to refill a prescription close to the time of the admission to the facility, ask the pharmacist to refill it in an amount that will supply your father until he enters the facility for the first day. The facility will order the medications from their contracted pharmacy. Reasons for using the facility's pharmacy are: first, to ensure safety in that the medications are the exact ones the physician ordered. The second reason is for ease of dispensing the medication. Each nurse that dispenses medications is responsible to give the correct medication and correct dose at the proper time. Each facility's medication routine helps to ensure safe distribution of medication. The State and Federal Government have strict guidelines for the storing and dispensing of medication to residents in health care facilities. Consult with the nurse regarding the facility's policy on administration of medications.

Q. What's the best way to let friends know my mother's address?

A. Family and friends mean so much to us. Notifying them of your mother's move to a nursing home will make them feel special. For those you cannot reach by phone, or if you want to send a reminder, send change of address cards found in your local card shops. If your mother enjoys writing letters, you will most assuredly want to notify her friends of the change of address.

Q. What's the best way for my father's mail to get to him?

A. Receiving and sending mail are obviously important. Prior to moving, you'll want to make some preparations. First, notify your father's current post office of his pending change of address and when it will become effective. They will inform you as to the amount of time they require to begin the change. Keep in mind that notifying the post office does nothing to communicate the new address to all the people sending mail. Therefore, you should begin to send out change of address cards to family, friends, magazines and newspapers, charge cards and any other senders of mail that your father still wants to continue receiving. Instead of going through this process you certainly could have a family member bring the mail to him. Although this will save you the time of having to send out change of address cards, it could be an inconvenience for a family member to bring the mail to him regularly. In addition, don't forget the enjoyment of getting mail daily, especially letters from family and friends and magazines that he will want to enjoy in a timely fashion.

Q. We'd like to have a party for our mother on her first day. Is that appropriate?

A. For many people, moving to an adult health care facility is a happy day. It is a kind gesture for a family to arrange a house warming party on the first day. Oftentimes people do not like the attention or the move is not a happy one. The bottom line is: any occasion that can bring family together to share in a special moment is a positive show of support. Many family members feel the need to express themselves in this manner as a way to cope with the change in their loved one's life. The decision regarding a party obviously depends on the circumstances within each family. If it will bring happiness to the day, then by all means have one. If a party is being planned, make sure you communicate with the staff at the new facility.

Q. On my aunt's first day, how many people should accompany her?

A. We all have someone who makes us feel safe and secure. This person or people may include a son, daughter, husband, wife, grandchild or best friend. Ask your aunt whom she would want with her on the first day. Make sure however, that you consider the number of people accompanying her. A large group can disrupt the admission process that is completed by the facility and distract the other residents. Keep the group small unless a party is being organized in a pre-designated room. An additional note: a pre-arranged departure time, once your aunt is admitted to the facility, should be established to reduce anxieties throughout her first day. It is often beneficial for family members to set their departure time around a key activity for the individual or the facility. Appropriate times are when meals are being served or when most residents are retiring to sleep.

Q. How will I know that the nursing home we have selected will stay at the level of quality that helped us select it initially?

A. The license for an adult health care facility is renewed by the State after an annual inspection. The review conducted by the State is public knowledge and can be easily accessed by calling the Department of Health Services. The Joint Commission on Accreditation of Hospitals (JCAHO) is an organization which maintains quality standards for health care organizations. Any facility that is JCAHO accredited is following a high standard for quality. Discuss this issue with the Director of Nursing and/or the Facility Administrator. Also, check with the Director of Nursing regarding the facility's resident council. This group represents the interests of the residents and helps to maintain the quality of their home.

Q. What kinds of questions can we expect to be asked by personnel at the nursing home we've selected?

A. The three (3) most common questions that most family members are not prepared to answer when asked are:

1) Should we resuscitate your loved one in the event of a medical emergency?
2) What funeral home is preferred?
3) Which family member will be the responsible party, the contact person in the event of an emergency?

These questions can be difficult to answer and can be difficult to discuss with your loved one. It is important information for the nursing staff to have in order to deliver complete individualized care. If these issues are too sensitive to discuss with your loved one, consult with your physician, nurse or the facility's social worker. These professionals can offer you direction for meeting with your loved one to obtain answers to the questions.

Terminology Made Easy

As with every industry there is unique terminology or language. The listing below contains commonly used words and phrases that you may come across:

- Activity of daily living: an activity often performed daily to maintain life. These activities include: dressing, bathing, toileting, preparing a meal, eating, handling finances, driving, using a telephone, shopping, taking medications, and housekeeping.

- Acute: a state of physical, psychological or emotional being that can be corrected or improved upon within a short period of time with care by a health care provider.

- Administrator's License: many adult health care facilities are administered by a state licensed professional who has completed a program and internship specifically designed for health care facilities. A current license tells you that this individual is qualified by the state to continue administration of that particular facility. An expired license means that this person is no longer licensed to practice in the state. Often times the administrator's license is visible in his/her office.

- Advanced Directive, Living will: a legal document indicating an individual's directions for health care in the event the individual is incapable of making health care decisions for himself/herself.

- Case conference: a meeting of health care providers involved in providing care to an individual. The conference is designed to communicate progress or non-progress of the individual according to the plan-of-care designed to meet the needs of the individual as agreed upon by the providers and the individual or responsible family member. Conferences for nursing home care are regulated and mandated by payor source providers and by nursing home licensing agencies.

- Certified Nurses Aide: a state certified individual who has completed training to assist individuals with the activities of daily living; duties are organized and supervised by a nurse.

- Chronic: a state of physical, psychological or emotional being that is long term and may or may not be alleviated by health care provided by a health care provider.

- Desire: a physical, mental, emotional, sexual and/or spiritual want of an individual that is not a necessity for survival yet when satisfied brings about a state of wellness or well-being.

- Health care: services given by a licensed medical professional in the areas of medicine, dentistry, psychiatry; services sought by an individual who wants assistance to correct a physical, mental, or emotional imbalance.

- Health care provider: a licensed professional with knowledge and experience in an area of health care serving an individual, family and/or community; care is regulated by a licensing agency usually a state department.

- Interventions: actions of a skilled health care provider to assist an individual towards a state of physical, psychological or emotional well-being as agreed upon by the individual and the provider.

- Joint Commission on Accreditation of Hospitals (JCAHO): a national accreditation organization for hospitals and health care organizations. Any facility that is accredited by JCAHO follows specific standards for delivering quality beneficial health care. Routine evaluations of accredited organizations are done to ensure that the standards are being maintained. JCAHO also directs participating organizations in meeting standards with alternatives and recommendations. Not all facilities are JCAHO accredited. Discuss with an administrator his/her reasons for not being accredited.

- Living Will: see Advanced Directive.

- Medicaid, state welfare health plan: a state program providing health care benefits to persons falling below a maximum allowable monthly and yearly income level. Many states recognize this plan as Medicaid while others, such as the state of California, recognize this plan under another name.

- Medicare: a federal health care system for citizens sixty-five (65) years old and older. Additional services can be purchased on a monthly basis. Services covered can include physician services, nursing services, laboratory and x-ray services, and a limited range of durable medical equipment. Medications are not usually covered. Persons under the age of sixty-five (65) who have been classified as "disabled" by a physician may

- Need: physical, mental, emotional, sexual and/or spiritual necessity of an individual that requires satisfying in order to maintain a status of wellness or well-being. qualify for Medicare disability which entitles them to early access to Medicare with some restrictions.

- Outcomes or goals: a specific desired state of wellness or being arrived upon by an individual requiring health care services with the assistance of a nurse or other health care provider and including the values, beliefs and desires of that individual and/or the responsible family member.

- Payer source: accessible funds to use towards the cost of health care. Sources for nursing home care coverage can include: Medicare, Medicaid, private or long-term care insurance and cash or out-of-pocket funds.

- Plan of Care: a personalized written plan designed by a nurse which includes physician orders, nursing interventions, and any interventions by other skilled care workers to meet health care outcomes or goals.

- Primary Care Nurse: the nurse responsible for managing the care of an individual.

- Resident: an individual residing in a skilled nursing care facility.

- Responsible family member: a family member or legal guardian who accepts responsibility for a person receiving care by a health care provider.

- Skilled care: health care requiring the services of a licensed health care professional.

- Transition: a point in time in which change occurs; the change may be physical, mental, emotional and/or spiritual; the transition is accompanied by a wide range of emotions which are dependent upon the meaning of the change to the individual.

- Union: in several health care facilities the nursing staff, including certified nurses aides, are organized by a union. This is typically seen in larger facilities. The dimension of quality care is not determined by the union, though unsettled union negotiations can affect a facility's staffing patterns. Questions concerning this issue can be directed to the Director of Nursing.

Places To Turn For Additional Information

Organizations

Organizations listed below can direct you to additional assistance at the State and/or local level:

Eldercare Locator   1112 16th Street
N.W. Suite 100
Washington, D.C. 20036
800-677-1116

The National Council on the Aging, Inc.
409 Third Street S.W.
Washington, D.C. 20024
202-479-1200

The National Association of Professional
Geriatric Care Managers   602/881-8008

The organizations below can be reached through your phone directory:

(State) Area Agency on Aging

(State) Office of the Ombudsman

(State) Department of Social Services - Programs for Elders or Seniors

(State) Elderly or Community Services Division

(State) Association of Health Care Facilities

(Local) Social Workers

Publications/Directories

Information normally found in your local library:

National Association for Home Care - National Home Care Directory
519 C Street
Stanton Park
Washington D.C. 20002
202-547-7424

Recommended Reading

Goldsmith, S.B. (1990). *Choosing A Nursing Home.* Prentice Hall Press.

Horner, J. (1982). That Time of Year - *A Chronicle of Life in a Nursing Home.* The University of Massachusetts Press.

Manning, D. (1985). *The Nursing Home Dilemma.* Harper & Rowe, Publishers.

Moss, F.E., & Halamandaris, V.J., (1977). *Too Old, Too Sick, Too Bad, Nursing Homes in America.* Aspen Systems Corporation.

Pieper, H.G. (1989). *The Nursing Home Primer.* Betterway Publications, Inc.

Siegal, A.P., & Siegal, R.S. (1993). *Forget Me Not.* Celestial Arts.

About the Author

Kathleen O'Toole, RN, BSN, serves as President of Adult Care Planning, Inc., an organization she founded in 1995. The goal of her organization is to assist individuals and families in identifying, understanding and selecting the best adult care service.

Mrs. O'Toole's expertise is in adult health and geriatrics with years of service working in nursing home, hospital and home health care environments. Through her career experiences, she identified the need to provide guidance to those trying to make difficult decisions in selecting adult care for themselves or a loved one. Mrs. O'Toole's career has given her first hand knowledge of the many adult care services available and the issues and emotions surrounding the selection process.

A native of North Carolina, Mrs. O'Toole received her nursing education in Connecticut and there developed her expertise in geriatrics. Currently living in California with her husband, Mrs. O'Toole continues her work with Adult Care Planning.